Editor-in-Chief and Founder:
  Lyndon H. LaRouche, Jr.
Editorial Board: *Lyndon H. LaRouche, Jr. , Helga Zepp-LaRouche, Robert Ingraham, Tony Papert, Gerald Rose, Dennis Small, Jeffrey Steinberg, William Wertz*
Co-Editors: *Robert Ingraham, Tony Papert*
Managing Editor: *Nancy Spannaus*
Technology: *Marsha Freeman*
Books: *Katherine Notley*
Ebooks: *Richard Burden*
Graphics: *Alan Yue*
Photos: *Stuart Lewis*
Circulation Manager: *Stanley Ezrol*

INTELLIGENCE DIRECTORS
Counterintelligence: *Jeffrey Steinberg, Michele Steinberg*
Economics: *John Hoefle, Marcia Merry Baker, Paul Gallagher*
History: *Anton Chaitkin*
Ibero-America: *Dennis Small*
Russia and Eastern Europe: *Rachel Douglas*
United States: *Debra Freeman*

INTERNATIONAL BUREAUS
Bogotá: *Miriam Redondo*
Berlin: *Rainer Apel*
Copenhagen: *Tom Gillesberg*
Houston: *Harley Schlanger*
Lima: *Sara Madueño*
Melbourne: *Robert Barwick*
Mexico City: *Gerardo Castilleja Chávez*
New Delhi: *Ramtanu Maitra*
Paris: *Christine Bierre*
Stockholm: *Ulf Sandmark*
United Nations, N.Y.C.: *Leni Rubinstein*
Washington, D.C.: *William Jones*
Wiesbaden: *Göran Haglund*

ON THE WEB
e-mail: eirns@larouchepub.com
www.larouchepub.com
www.executiveintelligencereview.com
www.larouchepub.com/eiw
Webmaster: *John Sigerson*
Assistant Webmaster: *George Hollis*
Editor, Arabic-language edition: *Hussein Askary*

EIR (ISSN 0273-6314) *is published weekly (50 issues), by EIR News Service, Inc., P.O. Box 17390, Washington, D.C. 20041-0390. (703) 777-9451*

European Headquarters: E.I.R. GmbH, Postfach Bahnstrasse 9a, D-65205, Wiesbaden, Germany
Tel: 49-611-73650
Homepage: http://www.eirna.com
e-mail: eirna@eirna.com
Director: Georg Neudecker

Montreal, Canada: 514-461-1557

Denmark: EIR - Danmark, Sankt Knuds Vej 11, basement left, DK-1903 Frederiksberg, Denmark.
Tel.: +45 35 43 60 40, Fax: +45 35 43 87 57. e-mail: eirdk@hotmail.com.

Mexico City: EIR, Sor Juana Inés de la Cruz 242-2 Col. Agricultura C.P. 11360 Delegación M. Hidalgo, México D.F.
Tel. (5525) 5318-2301
eirmexico@gmail.com

Canada Post Publication Sales Agreement #40683579

Postmaster: Send all address changes to *EIR*, P.O. Box 17390, Washington, D.C. 20041-0390.

Signed articles in *EIR* represent the views of the authors, and not necessarily those of the Editorial Board.

Victory Over Fraud

The Only Way You Can Win Is The Hard Way

May 5—In just a few words spoken over a few minutes on Tuesday evening, May 3, Lyndon LaRouche spelled out starkly what he himself has long known, and what every successful architect of victory has known,— but what others refuse to face. He showed that victory is only possible through doing the things that have never been done before,— indeed never even thought of before—based on a totally new original insight.

You can only win by doing what all the smart people knew was absolutely impossible. This is the story of the Inchon Landing of Sept. 15, 1950. MacArthur told the nay-sayers, namely the entirety of the U.S. high command, that "the very arguments you have made as to the impracticalities involved" confirmed his faith in the plan,— "for the enemy commander will reason that no one would be so brash as to make such an attempt." MacArthur finished his statement (like LaRouche, he knew when to finish), by whispering, "I can almost hear the ticking of the second-hand of destiny. We must act now or we will die. . . ."

But LaRouche's leadership has long been on a profounder level than even the genius MacArthur's. Better to think back to MacArthur's friend Gen.

> "The question is, how will Russia and China survive this situation? . . . this depends upon maneuvers on the part of the leading parties; that's the only chance. You cannot use deductive methods; they don't work. They can't work under these circumstances."

Charles de Gaulle. In his memoirs, de Gaulle recalled the moment in 1940 when all the French officials turned their back on his struggle against the treasonous "French" government at Vichy. "I felt like someone approaching the ocean," he wrote, "preparing to swim across."

(Yet he did swim across!)

This is almost impossibly difficult, but it can be done. It must be done, even if you can never say in advance how to do it. It has been done. And Lyndon LaRouche in particular has done it repeatedly and successfully. He debated and soundly defeated the chosen representative of the British system in 1971. Impossible! Then, later, through the Strategic Defense Initiative, he transformed the incoming U.S. Reagan Administration into the instrument of what would have been a new world system of peace and dramatic human progress. The British tried to assassinate Reagan, and went all-out to destroy LaRouche. They jailed him, but couldn't destroy him,— although his influence was effectively contained for years.

Achieving the Impossible While Under Attack

Yet even under this attack, LaRouche and his wife Helga succeeded in laying the basis for the Eurasian Landbridge/Silk Road policy and the BRICS, without which humanity would have no prospect for the future.

Beginning in October 2014, LaRouche set out again to accomplish the impossible. He outflanked the resistance and founded a new organization in Manhattan on a new basis, prominently including Classical choral work and competent Classical musical performance, both of which are linked to a weekly live dialogue with LaRouche. It seemed impossible; for years, every previous attempt had failed. But it is demonstrably succeeding and spinning off new organization on a new basis in Northern California, in Boston, and in a special way in Houston, Texas, where LaRouche leader Kesha Rogers has vigorously and effectively taken up the fight to revive the Space Program.

In the referenced Tuesday discussion, LaRouche also specified that, "Right now, the question is, how will Russia and China survive this situation? Because if they don't survive this situation, there is not going to be a civilization; it just won't happen. Now, this depends upon maneuvers and things of that nature on the part of the leading parties; that's the only chance. You cannot use deductive methods; they don't work. They can't work under these circumstances.

You actually are going to depend largely on a contributing factor in which Russia and China are going to play a controlling role. If they cannot successfully do that, then I think the case for humanity is poor; more than poor. In other words, it is not just this piece of equipment out there; it has to be the way in which this thing is orchestrated. And the orchestration has to come *chiefly*—chiefly, from Putin and from China, chiefly. And it will have to be an act of choice, chiefly; and it will be so clever, that it will take the enemy forces off their heels, before they can really come to an understanding of what they're being threatened by.

"It can be done; this kind of thing can be done. But it *has* to be done; or it doesn't work."

These thoughts touch on the most profound issues we know: One hopes that this account is truthful as far as it goes; it is not complete.

EIR Contents

www.larouchepub.com Volume 43, Number 20, May 13, 2016

RT

Cover This Week

A Classical music concert in Palmyra, Syria, organized by President Putin as a tribute to all victims of terror.

I. Murder in Manhattan

THE LESSON OF PALMYRA

September 11, 2001: The Time for Justice Is Now

by Diane Sare

May 8—In his May 5, 2016 Thursday night Fireside Chat, Lyndon LaRouche placed repeated emphasis on the events of September 11, 2001, which he had observed as they unfolded on that day of infamy:

Suddenly, two successive planes, which were actually captives from the Boston airport, the people on those planes were captured by terrorists, by trained terrorists, who committed suicide. They kept the people imprisoned in the plane, down to their arrival in the vicinity of Manhattan. And they circled around the building, and then the planes crashed into the specific towers.

I watched this personally. I watched the whole problem of this, from Boston airport to the circling of the other targets. Nobody ever took any hand, no one—that is no official ever took any hand—to efficiently prevent those crimes against our citizens in New York City in particular. None!

Other people also suffered, but these people were *marked out*. We're talking about a major part of the New York population was *murdered*, by the orders of the Queen of England and the orders of the Saudis! And there has been no justice ever delivered to the citizens of the United States on that account this far...

What happened, was *allowed* to happen, under the Presidency of the United States, to allow citizens of the United States, to be murdered *en masse* by the hands of Saudi agents, and with the consent of the Bush family. And the Bush family was the author of this process, his

FEMA News/Andrea Booher

9/11: the greatest evil ever perpetuated by the government of the United States, by the willing consent of people in the Presidency. Here, FEMA search and rescue teams clear rubble and search for survivors at the World Trade Center.

father and his role; and what of the British? Same way!

So when you're talking about this kind of case, of 9/11, when you're talking about that case, you're talking about the greatest, single, peculiar kind of evil, ever perpetuated *by the government* of the United States, or by the willing consent of other people in the Presidency and so forth...

There is no exaggeration. This thing was mass murder condoned by the U.S. government! Now when the U.S. government starts killing the majority of people in an area, *that's* the issue! Not some entertainment. Not some kind of interpretation. I know the details of that thing thoroughly. I know it back and forth. I was a witness to it, because I had an access to getting a view of what was going on. And I know what some of the international effects of this thing were. So, if someone comes up with this issue, you've got to say—don't say an explanation—say: *"This was a murder, a mass murder* of people in Manhattan." There is no explanation, there is no qualification, there is no quantification.

As a matter of fact, you have to make it *worse* than real, because of the implications of this: What do you think happens to people whose family members have been *murdered, mass murdered?* The fire department officials, mass murdered! And they were mass murdered! I know what the buildings were! I had walked through those buildings before the event occurred; I had lived at an earlier point in that area! I knew the thing *intimately*. And you cannot say *anything* good, *anything* productive, *anything* useful, which does not simply say, *these citizens of Manhattan were murdered by the consent of some officials of the U.S. government.*

Justice Must Be Done

How many Americans have given more than a passing thought to what occurred on that day, and to its aftermath? Who has thought about the hundreds of people on airplanes, traveling for business or family affairs, kidnapped by terrorists and smashed into their fiery deaths? What small or large heroic acts did each of them take in their final moments, from calling a loved one, or giving comfort to a terrified fellow passenger? What about the people who came in to work on that beautiful clear September morning at the World Trade Center or the Pentagon? Who were they? What contributions would each of them have made to mankind had they lived? What about the brave first responders, rushing to the scene, guiding injured people through the ashes and smoke to safety, and then returning to rescue more, only to die in collapsing buildings, or to die later because of poisons they inhaled on that fateful day?

What about our sons, daughters, husbands, and wives in the armed forces who have died in wars based upon lies? And who will think about all of the thousands upon thousands of men, women, and children killed abroad in these wars, while the actual organizers and financiers of the September 11, 2001 attacks have been protected by two successive administrations of the United States Government?

Now, either justice will be done, or we will all perish in the inferno of thermonuclear war—because the continuation of the crimes of September 11, 2001 will lead us there.

Even without the release of the carefully guarded 28 pages of the 9/11 Congressional Joint Inquiry, what is known about the attack is enough to land both George W. Bush, Barack Obama, and several members of their respective administrations in prison for the rest of their lives, had anyone in Congress the courage and integrity to pursue it.

For example, within days of the attack, it was known that 15 of the 19 hijackers who captured the planes were from Saudi Arabia. It is known that immediately following the attack, when supposedly no planes were allowed to fly, members of the Saudi Royal Family, as well as relatives of Osama Bin Laden, managed to be flown out of the United States back to Saudi Arabia and other locations. As former U.S. Senator Bob Graham—who chaired the Senate Select Committee on Intelligence and co-chaired the Joint Congressional Inquiry—has said repeatedly, many of these hijackers did not even speak English. Who helped them establish themselves here? Who paid their rent? Who organized and paid for their flying lessons?

Later it emerged that there were several key areas from which these hijackers operated. Among them are Sarasota, Florida; Paterson, New Jersey; San Diego, California; and Falls Church, Virginia. We know that when Senator Graham and others tried to pursue these leads, they were blocked by the FBI, as in the case of Sarasota, where the FBI denied there was anything of interest about a home in a gated community which had been visited on several occasions by lead hijacker Mohamed Atta and several of the other hijackers. Only recently, after an FOIA request from the *Broward Bulldog*, a local newspaper, did the FBI admit to having 80,000 pages of reports on investigations pertaining to that location.

How can it be that fifteen years after the mass murder of thousands of Americans on American soil, *not one member of Congress has demanded justice for these people? How can it be that the American people have allowed two successive Presidents of the United States to withhold the truth*, and not only to withhold the truth, but to act repeatedly to protect members of the Saudi Royal Family who are directly implicated in this crime? *Is this not treason?*

The 'Prayer for Palmyra'

Compare the treasonous cowardice shown by the leaders and citizens of the United States over the last fifteen years, to the actions taken recently by President Vladimir Putin of Russia. On May 5, President Putin organized a unique tribute, a *living memorial*, in honor of those who have died in the war against ISIS in Syria:

kremlin.ru

In contradistinction to the treasonous cowardice shown by the leaders and citizens of the United States over the last 15 years, Russian President Vladimir Putin on May 5 organized a Classical music concert in Palmyra, Syria, as a tribute to those who have died in the war against ISIS.

RT livestream coverage

Distinguished Russian conductor Valery Gergiev conducted the living memorial concert in a nearly 2000-year-old amphitheater in Palmyra, Syria, in which Isis had executed dozens of people.

The Palmyra concert, described by Putin as a tribute to all those fighting terrorism, opened with the Chaconne *for unaccompanied violin by Johann Sebastian Bach.*

A concert, directed by distinguished Russian conductor Valery Gergiev, was held in ancient amphitheater of Palmyra, an amphitheater nearly 2,000 years old, which ISIS had attempted to desecrate by executing dozens of people within its walls, including the archaeologist-custodian of the Palmyra ruins, 81-year-old Khaled al Asaad, who ISIS tortured and beheaded for refusing to reveal where he had hidden many treasured artifacts.

This "Prayer for Palmyra" paid homage to courageous individuals who have given their lives for the future of mankind, and implicitly to thousands of others slaughtered by ISIS. This extraordinary concert/prayer was described by Matt Ogden the next day on the LaRouche PAC Friday webcast:

Department of State

President Obama wanted no part of a true anti-terrorism coalition called for by Putin, and recently Obama's Secretary of State John Kerry demanded the ouster by Syrian President Assad by Aug. 2, setting up a strategic confrontation with Russia. Here, Secretary of State at the State Department daily press briefing, May 3.

The program yesterday in Palmyra was incredible. It was indescribable, really. The concert opened with the *Chaconne* by Johann Sebastian Bach for unaccompanied violin. The video footage of it is breathtaking, in aerial views that have the ruins of ancient Palmyra with the orchestra seated right in the middle, and one lone violin, playing this sublime piece by Johann Sebastian Bach.

This piece was followed by an excerpt from an opera by a modern Russian composer, Rodion Shchedrin. The opera is called *Not by Love Alone*. And then the final piece on the program was the First Symphony of the famous Russian composer Sergei Prokofiev. This is the work known as *The Classical Symphony*, a name that Prokofiev gave to it himself. He modelled it as his homage to the works of Haydn, Beethoven, and Mozart.

In the beginning of the event, Russian President Putin was streamed live into the amphitheater there, and delivered a prayer in which he situated the significance of this concert. He began by saying, "This concert should be a sign of our gratitude, remembrance, and hope." He said, "I see this as remembrance for all victims of terror, no matter the place and time, of crimes against humanity, and, of course, of hope, not just for the revival of Palmyra as a cultural asset of the whole of humanity, but for modern civilization, from this horrible fate of international terrorism. Today's action involved major inconvenience and dangers for everyone, being in a country at war, close to where hostilities are still ongoing. That has demanded great strength and personal courage from you all. Thank you very much."

Putin was *uniquely* qualified to make these remarks at this solemn occasion because it was his decision to act against ISIS, which he announced in September 2015, that led to the liberation of Palmyra and many other cities in Syria which had been captured and destroyed by the terrorist scourge. It should be remembered that when President Putin announced the formation of a true "anti-terrorism coalition," President Obama wanted no part of it, and even attempted to sabotage the Russian efforts by supplying the ISIS-supporting regimes of Turkey and Saudi Arabia with weapons and intelligence.

Alexander Gardner

President Abraham Lincoln took personal responsibility for those soldiers who had sacrificed their lives. His agony is seen in the Gettysburg Address. Here, Lincoln is meeting with his military leadership from the main eastern theater of the war, at the time of the Battle of Antietam, the bloodiest single-day battle in American history, 1862.

Just last week, Obama's Secretary of State John Kerry demanded Syrian President Assad's ouster by August 2, not only thus jeopardizing the fragile cease-fire, but putting the United States in a direct strategic confrontation with Russia. Under Obama, the United States is now allied with, arming, and supplying the very terrorists who murdered our own citizens on September 11, 2001.

Who Will Bring Justice?

If one takes a moment to reflect on the Gettysburg Address of American President Abraham Lincoln—who fought and defeated the British Empire in the so-called "Civil War" of the United States—the power, the wrenching emotional impact, of that dedication is to be found in the agony of a President Lincoln who took personal responsibility for those soldiers who had sacrificed their lives in the fight for freedom. He led our Republic to victory in the war, and himself paid the ultimate price when he was assassinated in 1865.

The disappearance of that morality of Lincoln from our present-day culture is the tragedy of the today's America. As Lyndon LaRouche stressed again in his Saturday Manhattan meeting, on the failure to respond to the attacks of September 11, 2001, "we do not have one, single, sign, of a thorough act of justice, in ac-

knowledgment of the condition of the people who died in that event."

This is not a time to "blame the government." It is a moment to look into one's own soul. Millions of Americans have allowed themselves to become "accessories after the fact" to our own government's complicity in the *mass murder* of 3,000 of our fellow citizens. We ourselves become criminals by condoning the crime, through our silence.

The great question of this moment is, "What are you, dear reader, going to do about this?"

Erdogan's Coup for Wider War In Southwest Asia

by Dean Andromidas

May 9—Turkish President Recep Tayyip Erdoğan, in forcing out Prime Minister Ahmed Davutoğlu, has removed the last internal obstacle to his consolidation of power, bringing Turkey one step closer to igniting a wider war in Southwest Asia. The move is a dangerous continuation of his Anglo-Saudi policy of supporting the overthrow of the Syrian government and sabotaging the efforts by Russian President Vladimir Putin and Foreign Minister Sergei Lavrov, in coordination with Secretary of State John Kerry, to end the war in the region.

Through a not-so-subtle manipulation of the executive council of the ruling Justice and Development Party, Erdoğan forced the resignation of Prime Minister Davutoğlu to consolidate his power as the sole authority in the state. On May 8, within 72 hours of the dumping Davutoğlu, Erdoğan ordered Turkish special forces to conduct its first incursion into Syria with U.S. and allied backing and assistance, including air strikes. According to the Daily *Yeni Safak*, known as a mouthpiece for Erdoğan, the sending of the 20-member commando team was only a prelude to establishing a "safe zone" along the Turkish border in Syrian territory.

Yeni Safak also reported that Turkey is planning to respond militarily against the Democratic Union Party

Turkish President Erdogan is threatening to expand Turkey's conflict with the Kurds into Kurdish areas in Syria and Iraq that border Turkey. Areas with Kurdish populations are shown in the map.

Creative Commons
President Recep Tayyip Erdoğan

Creative Commons
Former Turkish Foreign Minister Ahmet Davutoğlu

finance projects for the refugees, but Erdoğan wants the money transferred directly to the Turkish treasury.

Erdogan's Coup

Speaking at a news conference called by the main opposition Republican People's Party (CHP), party leader Kemal Kiliçdaroğlu charged: "Davutoğlu's resignation should not be perceived as an internal party issue; all democracy supporters must resist this palace coup."

Also denouncing the move as a coup, Peoples' Democratic Party (HDP) Co-chairman Selahattin Demirtaş declared that Davutoğlu was elected by the will of the people, but the "person at the palace wants to decide on who will rule this country. This is called a coup."

It is indeed a coup, since according to the Turkish Constitution, the President is the ceremonial head of state, and is supposed to withdraw from party politics and have nothing to do with who becomes prime minister.

Erdoğan declared openly that he is assuming the powers of an executive presidency even before any change in the Constitution. On May 6, one day after Davutoğlu stepped down, Erdoğan said, "At this point, there is no turning back. Everyone should accept this now." He said that it was "natural" for the party leadership to do as he wished, since he has been their "leader" for the last 12 years.

The chief editor of *Hurriyet*, Murat Yetkin, wrote May 6 that the dumping of Davutoğlu means, "A de facto shift to a semi-presidential system, where the prime minister effectively acts as the cabinet coordinator of the President."

In another commentary on May 9, Yetkin wrote, "That is also a very clear message to the outer world to show who the boss is in Turkey. From U.S. President Barack Obama to German Chancellor Angela Merkel and Russian President Vladimir Putin, from the United Nations to the European Union and international finance institutions, Erdoğan is sending the message that

(PYD), the Syrian Kurdish militia backed by Russia and the West, including the United States, if the PYD hits Turkish soil, or poses any threat to Turkey's border, or to its security more generally.

It reports that if the government finds evidence that the PYD is attacking Turkish territory, including in cooperation with the Kurdistan Workers' Party (PKK), Turkish forces will apply the rules of engagement and will strike PYD targets in Syria.

Erdoğan could also throw the hapless Europeans into disarray once again by reopening the refugee floodgates.

Erdoğan is threatening to cancel Turkey's agreement with the European Union (EU) on refugees, if the EU demands a change in Turkey's broad terrorism law. Erdogan is using this issue to go after his internal political opposition.

Threatening the Europeans, Erdoğan said, "If there is a[n additional] condition, there is no deal." He added, "You can go and make a deal [with] whoever you like."

Hurriyet senior commentator Yusuf Kanli warned May 9 that these statements should "be taken very seriously by Europe ... if he said he will dump the deal if his conditions are not met, he will surely dump it. Is Europe ready for a new flood of Syrian, Iraqi, Asian, and African refugees? What comes first for Europe, its interests, or norms and values? Europe must decide."

Part of that deal is €6 billion which is supposed to

RT

The devastation of the Kurdish town of Cizre in Turkey, resulting from fighting between the Turkish government and Kurdish fighters. Cizre is on the Tigris River, and on the border with Syria.

there is one and only one address to talk to in Turkey and that is the President, himself."

Although Davutoğlu was hand-picked by Erdoğan as prime minister in 2014 when Erdoğan became President, he has been accused of not fully carrying out Erdoğan's wishes, especially his demand that a change in the Constitution be forced through parliament, or accomplished through a referendum, to enable him to acquire executive powers officially.

In listing the conflicts between Erdoğan and Davutoğlu, *Hurriyet* pointed to Davutoğlu's scheduled meeting with U.S. President Barack Obama and Vice President Joe Biden, which was to have taken place the same week he was forced out. It was officially canceled because the White House claimed the President's schedule was too crowded, but in fact, Erdoğan let it be known to his friend in the White House that he opposed the meeting and Obama obliged. There is little doubt that the Kerry-Lavrov Syrian ceasefire and transition policy were to be on top of the agenda. The question to ask is whether Erdogan and Obama acted to sabotage the efforts of Kerry by getting Davutoğlu out.

The new prime minister will not be named until the ruling Justice and Development Party holds a special party congress on May 22, when a new party leader will be elected. There is a long list of possibilities, including Energy Minister Berat Albayrak, Erdoğan's son-in-law. All have one thing in common. They owe their political careers to Erdoğan.

Turkey As Anglo-Saudi Marcher Lord

There were signs for weeks that Davutoğlu was attempting to shift Turkish policy towards sanity. Not that he had lost his Muslim Brotherhood credentials, but Erdoğan's insane policies have bought catastrophe onto Turkey itself.

It should be remembered that in 2003, Davutoğlu, who was then foreign minister—along with former President and Prime Minister Abdullah Gul—opposed Turkey's entry into the war against Iraq launched by President George W. Bush and Vice President Dick Cheney, and managed to carry with him enough AKP members of parliament to prevent Turkey's entry into the war. By contrast, Erdoğan wanted Turkey not only to back the war, but to send Turkish troops into northern Iraq. The fact that Turkey did not enter the war enabled it to enjoy almost ten years of peace.

Unlike in 2003, Erdoğan in 2013 brought Turkey fully behind the operation to overthrow the Syrian government, bringing upon Turkey the disaster it avoided in 2003.

Because of that decision, the country is beginning to look like Iraq. Erdoğan's support for the Syrian opposition—including backing the terrorist Al-Nusra Front and sending Turkish (ostensibly ethnic Turkmen) fighters into Syria—has caused a massive blow-back into Turkey. Deadly suicide bombings seem to be taking place every week, including in the capital, Ankara, and Istanbul, the country's largest city and major tourist venue, bringing tourism to a standstill. The shooting down of a Russian war plane last November has brought Russian sanctions down on Turkey, leading to a collapse of agricultural exports to Russia and reducing

Russian tourism to nearly zero. The economy is beginning to tank because of the perceived instability, and long-term private investment, not just foreign investment, has reportedly collapsed.

The cities in the predominantly Kurdish regions in Turkey's South East are already looking like Syria's war-torn Aleppo. There are now no less than 500,000 internal refugees in Turkey, refugees who have fled cities in Turkey's South East that have become battle-grounds between Turkish security forces and the PKK.

All of this is the result of Erdoğan's policy of turning Turkey into the marcher lord for the Anglo-Saudi Sunni alliance, not just against Syria, but also against Egypt and Iran. In the last six months, Erdogan has consolidated a military alliance with Saudi Arabia and Qatar.

Erdoğan's obsession with resurrecting the "grandeur" of the Ottoman Empire has seen him bring Turkey into the center of the politics of the Arab region and into direct alliance with Saudi Arabia.

Erdoğan has been a frequent traveler to the Saudi Kingdom, both as prime minister and President, to ingratiate himself at the feet of the House of Saud. It is well known that the billions of Saudi petrodollars pouring into Turkey enabled Erdoğan to repeatedly win elections.

When Obama went to Saudi Arabia last month, he was met at the airport by the equivalent of the mayor of Riyadh. But the Saudi King himself greeted Erdoğan at the airport when he made an official visit in December 2015. The Sultan and the King hammered out what they called a Strategic Cooperation Agreement, including a mutual security pact that includes joint military exercises and even holding joint cabinet meetings at least twice a year.

These arrangements were solidified by subsequent visits to Riyadh by Prime Minister Davutoğlu and King Salman's official visit to Turkey in April, when Erdoğan bestowed on the King the Order of State of the Republic, Turkey's highest honor for a foreigner, while praising him to the heavens as a deliverer of peace throughout Southwest Asia. Saudi Arabia's idea of creating a NATO-style alliance of Arab states was also said to have been on the agenda.

Of course the target of such an alliance would be Iran: Erdoğan listens closely to the Saudi position on the issue. When Erdogan made his official visit to Iran in April 2015, he made sure to meet Saudi Crown Prince Mohammed bin Nayef in Ankara just a few hours before his departure for Tehran.

Since Erdoğan is not satisfied with the billions he gets from the Saudis, he has been cultivating ties with Qatar, the principal supporter of the Muslim Brotherhood. These efforts have led not only to more billions flowing into Turkey, but also to military cooperation. Last April, following a two-day visit to Qatar by then Prime Minister Davutoğlu, a military agreement was signed for the deployment of the Turkish Armed Forces in Qatar.

The agreement, signed by Turkish Defense Minister Ismet Yilmaz and his Qatari counterpart, Khalid bin Mohammad al-Attiyah, calls for a military base to be built in Qatar, the first Turkish military facility in the region, which is expected to be ready within two years.

Foreign troops are only needed in Qatar and Saudi Arabia to protect the governments from their own populations, or to fight Iran if the Anglo-Saudi alliance should launch such a war. Erdoğan has become a very dangerous man for all of Southwest Asia.

II. No More Frauds

To Present a Solution of Something Not Considered Before!

This is an edited transcript of Lyndon LaRouche's Dialogue with the Manhattan Project on Saturday, May 7, 2016.

Question: Good afternoon, Mr. LaRouche. Obama and his ilk have been mocking Putin, saying that Putin is trying to portray himself as this big leader, a big man, trying to portray himself as a force of good in the world. And that the United States really is the power in the world, and we are the ones that really are going to defeat ISIS, and we're doing all these wonderful things to fight terrorism.

I want to bring everyone's attention to that situation, where we know that Obama has sent in 250 military personnel. He doesn't call them "boots on the ground." He calls them "military personnel," so they can't possibly be "troops," without the consent of Congress. So, again, he's kind of slipped by that one.

I also want to bring everyone's attention what you had to say under the picture of the amphitheater. I'm not going to read it out loud, but everyone can read it. It's quite wonderful; it concerns the Classical music composition, and how

The human individual is not an animal, but today most human beings treat their own species as animals. Above, the German scientist Bernhard Riemann. His breakthroughs made the later advances of Albert Einstein possible.

we need this uplifting, and this wonderful optimism, at a time when our world could end, very abruptly.

Could comment on that, please?

LaRouche: I can tell you, that anything that's intelligent, which is done by an intelligent person, *would be something which would be a challenge to any audience, because it would present a solution, of something which had not been considered before.* That's the whole idea. The meaning of existence, the meaning of what we can accomplish, is something which has to be placed in the right place.

The Meaning of 'Human'

Question: We are close to the anniversary of Alan Shepard going into space, and about a month ago we had the anniversary of Yuri Alekseyevich Gagarin orbiting the planet. Now, 55 years later, in some sense progress has been suspended. When it comes to the human species, you either progress, or you head for annihilation. And we have the threat of nuclear war, but also the extinction of the sense of progress and development, in the species.

You've called for a space program; Kesha Rogers has

been organizing for this. I think in some ways the deep importance of it, in the sense that this is the evolution of the human species, it would have to be a crucial part of a Renaissance. Not only should Americans recognize this, but this is something that is at the core of our ability to succeed.

I want to ask you if you have more? And also this idea that we should be recognizing that this was the end of progress. Obama, of course, has had the role of finishing it off, or trying to. So, I want to see what thoughts you have.

LaRouche: What mankind is going to be able to do, is to discover the meaning of the birth of human beings. Now, the problem today is that most human beings have no mark of distinction. They're simply things that were dropped into the case, and therefore, you just simply went along; to *sing along*, as if to sing along. And that is not what you need.

What you need is to understand that the human individual is not an animal. Now, most people treat human beings as animals; they believe they are animals. The fact that they talk does not detract from that. So therefore, they don't understand the meaning of "human." Most human beings, today, *do not know the meaning of human*. The difference of human from monkey, for example; they don't really know the difference. They recognize there is a distinction, but they don't know what the distinction means.

So therefore, their problem is: What is the source of human existence?

Human existence lies in the Solar System and beyond the Solar System. And, it's in those areas that mankind is able to reach a voice, which reaches into a more creative form of existence. In other words, the

CC/Paul Wiesinger

Johannes Kepler made breakthroughs which got people to think in ways that had previously not been considered normal. Here, a statue of Kepler in Linz, Germany.

baby is not just born, but the baby is given an ability to develop the baby's own abilities and futures.

In other words, a great scientist will actually create the idea of the subject matter. And so therefore, the point is to get human beings to be able to think in terms that normal human beings cannot; and one way is going into space, going into service in space. That's one way to do it. The skill to do that, on command, is very important.

And therefore, when you really get at this thing—You want to get at it? Get at the future! And, that's the way you have to do it. You say, "What is this? I'm not a baby. But I have a future, and I'm going to express a future, and I'm going to find a way to do that. So I will do something so that a parent is astonished, because the child knows better than the parent."

Question: Good afternoon, Mr. LaRouche. R— from Brooklyn. In reading *EIR*, I see why you dislike Bertrand Russell. His writings and ideas through the Truman administration and the FBI dealt a death-blow to this republic, especially our educational system. Would you care to put more gasoline on the fire?

LaRouche: [Laughs] Well, I don't like to throw gasoline on fire all over the place. That is not one of my intentions.

I would say, no, the point is we have to understand exactly how people become stupid enough to make those mistakes. And we have to chide them and remind them, "Where did *you* go to school?" or "Where *didn't* you go to school?" and that's the way to approach it or to reply to that.

Question: [follow-up] The way the current universities are teaching history, I doubt if most people even know that Bertrand Russell existed, and what his effect on this society has been.

LaRouche: I'm afraid that all too many people remember Bertrand Russell. They should never have remembered him at all! [Laughter] So anyway, there's no hope for anything about Bertrand Russell—nothing! There's nothing good about him and never will be, and he's still rotting in his grave. It's not really something that we want to waste our time on. He's waste matter.

The Fraud Against Einstein

Question: I want to ask you your take on why Einstein had an approach to the composition of the universe, that gave him the ability to hypothesize gravitational waves. I wanted to offer two other ideas on this: One is that it's amazing to me that for 100 years there was an attempt to demonstrate whether that was true or not, because that's a long time to concentrate on this hypothesis. But now we have this verification and you have the idea that Einstein had this concept 100 years ago, basically, and his idea of the composition of the universe.

So I want to ask you what you thought about Einstein's approach that gave him this concept of the structure of the universe itself, that we're now seeing demonstrated in this way?

LaRouche: What happened is that, in his life, there are a number of things which he did that were rejected by the majority of the scientific community. And what has happened in the intervening hundred years, is that he was right and they were wrong. The question is, why did they do the thing that was wrong? Why? Because they were suckers, and it's an all-day sucker or something like that. That's what they were, they were suckers.

See, the point is, people are always trying to get a deductive approach to things which are important, important enough to attract attention. And that he had a correct understanding of the way to approach developments in space. He was right. *They were wrong.* In other words, it wasn't a case of people being out there, making a sudden discovery innocently. Everything that was charged against him in this respect, was a fraud *against* him. And finally the fraud got to squeaking so loud that nobody could deny it after a century.

And what happened is, a century later, they had a fraud on their hands, not a croaking fraud but a different

During Einstein's life, much of his work as a theoretical physicist was rejected by the majority of the scientific community, and he was denied teaching positions throughout Europe. The last one hundred years has proved that he was right and they were wrong. He initially worked in the Swiss Patent Office where this photo was taken in 1905.

kind of fraud. It was always a fraud. He made the discovery; he defined the discovery. He laid out the characteristics of the discovery. Then, a century later they say, "I dunno how this happened," or something like that.

Einstein was unique, and what you find is that most people in science, in physical science, do not understand physical science. Why? Because they do not want to offend the people who are making up the bad stories.

Question: [follow-up] I want to ask about your proposal that Kesha and the organization launch a big fight to revive the space program, and about the way this would impact people's ability to understand the universe, to make breakthroughs—the average citizen. That is what you saw in the early stages of the space program and how important that is in reviving a culture, a commitment to production and scientific advancement among average people.

U.S. Air Force/Melanie Rodgers Cox

NASA administrator Gene Kranz proposed, in response to the cancellation of the later Apollo missions, a Moon shot to the far side of the Moon to fire the imagination of the American people.

The Chinese are talking now about going to the far side of the Moon and what can be discovered by doing so, and how that would be transmitted to the population at large. It was pointed out to me that Gene Kranz, one of the famous NASA administrators, in 1972, in his book he talks about a big discussion among scientists about what to do with the shutdown of the later Apollo missions. And in 1972, Gene Kranz said, "Well, we've got to grab the imagination of the American population for space. Why don't we go to the far side of the Moon?" And Kranz said in his book, we had the capability to do it in 1972.

So now the Chinese are doing it, or they're proposing to do it, again, to achieve it, but also to grab the imagination of people. It seems that this idea that you have to grab the imagination of the people, to move the program, is critical, and it relates to what Einstein did, because what do we now know about the universe that we didn't know before, and can that be communicated to inspire the average American?

LaRouche: That's a difficult thing to spin that way. Yes, that happens; things like that happen. But what's the authority on which to define the success of such a program? That's the question. And this means—what has happened along the way? It's not a question of discovery in the ordinary, silly sense of discovery—not that sense at all. The point is that there's a recognition that there is something missing in the process. Something is already missing. Now people having found themselves holding something up, which is missing,

and looking for it; now they make a discovery. But the discovery is that while they're sitting out there, they suddenly—"Oh, I'm a genius, I just had some kind of a sexual experience or something which made me very happy." Something like that.

No, this is not anything of that type. The point is, *mankind is ignorant of his own knowledge!* And these people who go out there and say these things and say this is my discovery, *my discovery*, it's not their discovery. They don't know what they're talking about. And even the people who are doing this thing, on the so-called "discovery" of Einstein's gravitational waves, that's nonsense, absolute nonsense! It's a way of trying to cover up what they were trying to hide.

Real Intelligence

Dennis Speed: Lyn, I remember you telling me a story—this was in 1973, about how you used to go up to Malcolm X's talks—I don't know if it was at the Audubon Ballroom or where it was—and you heard him in Harlem, and what he would do in the individual talks … And he would imitate the pimps, the prostitutes, the various other characters, the drunks; and what would happen is, people would at first be uncomfortable and then they would begin to laugh, uproariously, and then he would turn to them and say, "You see what you're like?!"

"You see what you're like?"—that is the core of real intelligence. That's what made Malcolm important, and that's what's missing from this issue, when people talk about things like Einstein and the gravitational waves. Now, you have attacked Bertrand Russell continually as the most evil man of the 20th Century. People then say, "Oh, what does that mean? Do we have to look at this *Four Essays on Philosophy*, do we have to look at what he said about Riemann? Do we…?" And you just said: Look, the whole way that people are talking about discovery, about thought—all of this is a game, it's a fraud. It doesn't work this way. You're being, as Malcolm used to say, "You been took, you've been bamboozled, you've been baffled."

And what I'm reminded of, and what you're laying out here now, is you see, last week when you spoke here, and you laid out this whole thing about the FBI, there was real, real awe —meaning terror, as well as admiration—but like, "Yeah, well, maybe he can do that, but I don't know, I mean, is this really what we're all supposed to do?"

And I'm saying this, because this issue of our actions in Manhattan and the way in which you understand how ideas and intelligence work—to me, I think, that is what I'm hearing from you.

LaRouche: Well, I always have been very opposed to my parents, and to almost everybody else that I was associated with, because I had known very quickly that they were wrong. So, when you go through life knowing that the people who are trying to teach you something are wrong, that has an effect. And I found that I had some things that I had discovered, and these other guys didn't know what they were talking about. But I did.

If you want to be educated in schools, by and large, with some exceptional cases, people will not be able to recognize what the truth is. Most of the population does not have the ability to distinguish the truth from fraud. But when somebody helps them and comes along and gives them an explanation, and they go through it and begin to re-examine their notions, that is when you get that kind of an effect.

Speed: You were able, in the period 1970, 1971, 1972, to pull a bunch of us out of campuses, in which this sort of fraud was not only practiced, it had been nearly perfected. And it was sort of nonstop fraud. And we used to like watching you deal with these people, which I think is how a certain disposition was passed on to some of us; because it was fun, it was great to do ... Now, here's what I want to know from you: How do we go about creating that disposition, where people like the idea of actually beating up, destroying fraud?

LaRouche: Well, Manhattan was a very peculiar kind of environment in those days, but you would have people who would actually do that, as I would do it, and did it in schools earlier—recognize the thing is a fraud. In other words, they were laying out a solemn foundation for a great discovery, or something like that. And you turn around, and you look around and you say, "where'd this damned idiot come from?"

And so we would have people in a community, Manhattan in part, other places, and internationally also, and we would succeed in making discoveries. And we made the discoveries by rejecting the opinions of foolish people.

Furtwängler Revived in Manhattan

by Dennis Speed

The article is followed by two extended notes and a dialogue transcript—on the Radio Research Project, Furtwängler, and the teaching of voice placement, respectively—that amplify its thrust.

May 9—The conductor Wilhelm Furtwängler, though deceased since 1954, is about to begin a belated residency in Manhattan. The LaRouche Manhattan Project, through a series of discussions, "music-evenings," and larger musical performances for New York City audiences numbering in the hundreds, intends to correct the crime against the American people committed by the

Wilhelm Furtwängler was extensively vilified by the Nazi leadership, and in the United States, which resulted in the rejection of his 1936 appointment to head the New York Philharmonic.

post-FDR Truman-era British Intelligence operation known as the Congress for Cultural Freedom (CCF). Through this institution, countless minds were destroyed, creativity was attacked and then abolished, and madness, in the form of arbitrary "taste" and "trends," has come increasingly to dominate every aspect of American thought. Recently, however, the disgust for the sociopathic behavior on exhibit from a combination of Obama's White House and the apparently inevitable alternative of either a Hillary Clinton or Donald Trump-led Presidency, has caused moral panic to register among even the most recalcitrant.

Rectification of the criminal injustice done by agencies including the FBI, in the collusion to mask from the American people the truth behind the murder of the more than 3,000 Americans killed 15 years ago at the World Trade Center, requires a moral fortitude and courage to concentrate on the objective of Justice, that is identical with what it actually takes to perform a symphonic composition by Beethoven properly. The fact that Americans were denied the presence of Furtwängler in New York City both in 1936 and in 1951, as a conductor and teacher, contributed directly to the toleration of the Truman era, the McCarthy era, and the creation in that time of American Modernism in the arts.

Only by reversing the rule of the arbitrary in American musical practice—a mission that the Schiller Institute was induced by LaRouche to take up in the 1980s with the campaign for all Classical music to be performed at the "Verdi tuning" of A=432—is it possible to return to a sense of proportion—of Justice—in any sector of American life. The moral illiteracy of the population can only be fought with a resurgence—a *Risorgimento*—of true, good singing as a widespread and coveted practice.

Furtwängler would have picked up the baton dropped, not by Arturo Toscanini in 1936, but by Antonin Dvorak in 1895 when, after a failed but glorious attempt to establish the Manhattan-based National Conservatory of Music with musician and philanthropist Jeanette Thurber, he returned to Czechoslovakia, defeated by the then dominant segregationists of the American South and their co-thinkers in the North. (Johannes Brahms had personally supported Dvorak in this effort, including Dvorak's championing of the Negro Spiritual as the basis for "a great and noble school of music.") Although Thurber lived until 1945, and would have been able to reactivate part of her project had Furtwängler been placed at the head of the New York Philharmonic in 1936-37, that was not to be. The mastery of the idea of motivic thorough-composition characteristic of Brahms, and his protege and collaborator Dvorak, still existed in the performance practice of Furtwängler, also a composer. This was the possibility that was stopped, and the CCF "Dark Age" substituted in the aftermath of Roosevelt's death.

Two Voices

We cannot competently discuss the idea of motivic thorough-composition here, but we can identify how Furtwängler thought about creativity in musical performance in his own words. "Let us consider the activity of artistic creation. When we look more closely at this process, we find we can distinguish two levels. On the first, each individual element combines with those adjacent to it to form larger elements, these larger elements then combining with others and so on, a logical outwards growth from the part to the whole. On the other level, the situation is the reverse: the given unity of the whole controls the behavior of the individual elements within it, down to the smallest detail. The essential thing to observe is that in any genuine work of art, these two levels complement each other, so that the one only becomes effective when put together with the other."

In a conversation with colleagues, reflecting upon the quality of musicianship of his friend the late Norbert Brainin, principal violinist of the Amadeus Quartet, Lyndon LaRouche once remarked that "you have to

place the ideas, in the way you perform. Or how you hear them. and you have to place those ideas. Musical training will not do it. A more spiritual quality has to be added to it, or else it doesn't work. It's a failure. It's very difficult, because the standard became more and more the standard of the mechanical performance, and that loses it, the person performing is losing the connection to the principle. Something must be caused to radiate *inside you*, in the relationship to an important performance. There has to be something inside you that's controlling the way you respond. and the way you perform. That's the most important thing. That's why I don't want any kind of popular music; I don't want it! I don't want it in my presence. I fear it will destroy my soul! That's the way I feel about it. You have to approach everything that way. You have to,— by approaching yourself that way, you maintain and secure the quality of morals that you should have anyway. The pragmatist is always the damn fool, a nuisance."

The identity in intention of the two voices should be clear.

At the center of the Schiller Institute's Manhattan Project lies the rejoining of a battle that that organization had brought to New York City in the late 1980s. At that time the Institute, at the epistemological instigation of Lyndon LaRouche, issued the *Manual on Tuning and Registration*, a groundbreaking and still unsurpassed argument for the proper tuning of music, based on an accurate understanding of the unique role of the Italian *bel canto* method of voice placement that is the basis for all beautiful vocal production in all languages. The cultural relativists of a quarter century ago went wild; the battle was joined.

What was not realized by those unaware of the deeper issues, was that this was cultural warfare on the highest of levels. It was this battle that had been fought by conductor Wilhelm Furtwängler, in fact, against the Nazi regime. It was a battle of truth against pragmatic adaptation to the "triumph of the arbitrary will" over science, culture, society, and man. For example, it had been the Nazi Joseph Goebbels who had decreed, at a conference that he had organized in 1939, that what was widely referred to as "the scientific pitch" of A=432 would be changed to A=440, ostensibly for radio broadcasting and other purposes. Beyond the apparent "technical" surface of that matter lay an attempt to deny the physical laws, not only of the human voice, but of the universe itself, and the consequences of ignoring the same.

The Choral Principle

The *Manual on Tuning and Registration* exposed, in 1988, that "The influence of Marxist and kindred social theories among musicologists, and others, has produced the popularization of a doctrine to the effect, that modern composers belong to successive periods of musical mannerisms and tastes, such as the Baroque, Rococo, Classical, Romantic, and Modernist. The spread of this social theory has been perhaps the chief reason the majority of professional musicians no longer grasp some among the most rudimentary features of principles of Classical musical composition."

The "tuning question" however, is no different than that of the destruction of science starting in about the year 1900 throughout Europe. It is the task of the LaRouche Manhattan Project to return to science, to the "scientific," that is, proper tuning, and to thereby champion the actual spirit of the compositions to be presented. First, this means performing only at the proper tuning of C=256 cycles per second (cps). Second, this means going "beyond the notes," "behind the notes," and "in between the notes," as Furtwängler instructed. Music is not contained in notes, just as ideas are not contained in words.

It is the imposition of the false belief that the opposite is true, that is the "first cause" of the woeful political choices and policy options that confront America's citizens today. They are powerless, without music, to reverse these non-choices and evil, anti-human policies, in the wake of the "New Dark Age" culture that the Obama and Bush Administrations have embodied; they cannot hope to, and will not, find any "political" remedy, limited in this way, no matter what they do. That is because they believe that their pre-determined cultural choices are freely chosen by them, the way they believe that they pick a box of detergent at the not-so-supermarket. They at their best demand to fail to recognize, and at their worst vehemently reject, the ugly truth about their ugly culture: It was given to us to wear, and it is up to us to divest ourselves of it, to "un-slave" ourselves, to refuse to put the shackles on ourselves at night after a long day spent at the wage-slavery and debt-slavery that most people mistakenly call "employment," or, even later, after the even more degrading, often borderline-criminal or actually criminal activity we un-ironically call "entertainment."

Beyond the musical performances that the Manhattan project has conducted, and the choruses that are now meeting as part of that project, the central pedagogical activity devoted to the task of mental/musical un-enslavement, is the *solfège* class being conducted by Diane Sare, founder and co-leader of the Schiller Institute New York Community Chorus. Prior to each Saturday dialogue with LaRouche, Sare invites the audience to investigate Wilhelm Furtwängler's idea of musical performance and comprehension. This is done not by merely *listening* to Furtwängler's 1953 recorded performance of the Schubert Ninth Symphony; instead the audience is required to *sing* the piece, as a chorus, and to work through it, using *solfège*. Further, the *solfège* system used is that of a "fixed *do*," where the syllable "*do*" always falls at the musical tone C, instead of the "movable *do*," a much more generally taught and relatively arbitrary system in which the key of the piece—A Flat, D Minor, F Sharp—is taken as the "*do*" starting point. In this approach, instead of the banal "music appreciation" that rendered people defenseless in the 1960s against the onslaught of noise, the audience/chorus participates in a musical laboratory intended not to convince them that "Classical music is good for you," but that the idea of composition, according to Classical principles, is both accessible to their minds, and at the same time is *not* the way that they generally choose to think. It is the ability of the participants to increasingly appreciate the tragic nature of their generally wrong pathway of choice in what is mistakenly called "the real world" which is the goal of this spiritual exercise. And from this standpoint, real deliberation begins.

American Romanticism

Rescuing the American mind from the disease of Romanticism, as the poet Heinrich Heine so scathingly characterized it in his book-length study, *The Romantic School*, may be the only means left, in the short term, to reverse the descent into babbling obscenity, tinged with lunacy, that has threatened to become the norm in American political discourse with the advent of the nearlyunbelievable Donald Trump campaign. This were most efficiently done by reacquainting American children and young adults with the vocal practices of *bel canto* singing. Yet, this cannot be presented, truthfully, as a "thing in itself." The political reason for the suppression of this knowledge must also be communicated.

The fraud of "periods of European musical history" must be exposed to the student as well. The *Manual* states: "It is usually assumed that the 'Romantic Period' erupted on the European continent during the period of the 1815 Treaty of Vienna and the anti-Classical Carlsbad Decrees. For that reason, all leading composers after 1827-28 (the years of the deaths of Beethoven and Schubert, respectively) are not only classed as representatives of the Romantic Period; in most instances of what passes for standards of performance of the musical repertoire today, the works of strictly 'Bachian' composers such as Schubert, Mendelssohn, Chopin, Schumann, and Brahms are interpreted in a way more or less appropriate for Hector Berlioz (1803-1869), Liszt, Wagner, and Hugo Wolf (1860-1903)."

In today's high school and lower classrooms in America, there is little danger of the student having to be weaned from this mistaken idea, since "classical," if it means anything at all, usually refers to the Beatles and their musical kin, or if the student is a true archaeologist, the "big band" era of the 1930s and 1940s.

It must be pointed out that American conductor Leonard Bernstein didn't help matters much; he contributed mightily to this state of affairs. Though he performed an important, self-redemptive service after the November 1989 fall of the Berlin Wall in his December performance of the Beethoven Ninth Symphony, Lenny's Romanticism was the Trojan Horse upon whose back the FBI-CIA "thought-police" rode the 1960s counter-culture through the music departments of every university, and through every conservatory in the United States. This is approximately the 50th anniversary of Bernstein's 1967 "Heart of Darkness" television broadcast calling for the Classical music world to embrace T.W. Adorno's Princeton-based Radio Research Project and the transition of the CCF (just then being exposed as CIA) from its State Department sponsored 1950s/1960s advocacy of "jazz" to the new British Intelligence branch-project called "rock."

Bernstein, to be fair, had himself been targeted by the CCF, including in its first intervention, at the "Cultural and Scientific Conference for World Peace," held at the Waldorf Astoria on March 25, 1949. The disruption was led the CIA-funded Sidney Hook, who in the 1970s was a major enemy of Lyndon LaRouche personally, and LaRouche's campaign against what LaRouche then called the "quackademics" in American economics, history, and political science departments, including Hook's University Center for Rational Alternatives (UCRA). Bernstein and 49 others were featured in Henry Luce's *Life* magazine, with large passport-style photographs. Along with Leonard Bernstein, Albert Einstein, Clifford Odets, Frank Lloyd Wright, Aaron Copland, and Henry Wallace were some of the others characterized by the magazine as "dupes of the Kremlin."

Bernstein often repeated the phrase, "But I like it," in the 1967 "Inside the Rock Revolution" program, in which he even refers to several of the Beatles records as "important compositions," calling to mind the chilling last sentence of George Orwell's *1984*: "He loved Big Brother." Terrorized ever since the late 1940s, and in the New York City that was terrorized into rejecting Furtwängler, Lenny clearly not only knew better, but had chosen to embrace the worse.

Sometimes, even many times, the Good appears to be defeated by its opposite. It need not be so. After the rejection of his 1936 appointment to head the New York Philharmonic upon Arturo Toscanini's departure, and after Furtwängler's extensive vilification during the Second World War, a final attempt to bring Furtwängler to New York City in 1951 on the part of Rudolf Bing and others, failed in turn. The terror atmosphere of that time proved to be too much. But there is more than one way to defy the Inquisition, the FBI, and British (Un-) Intelligence. Furtwängler will now, in 2016, take up residence in Manhattan among those who care about, and are prepared to defend truth. The Manhattan project can succeed in this. Musical and Classical artistic truth, once crushed to the earth, can and will rise again.

The Radio Research Project

The war against Classical culture in music in the United States escalated dramatically in the 1930s. The Radio Research Project, funded by the Rockefeller Foundation—starting in 1937 as a national venture to study the effect of what was about to be termed "mass media," and headquartered at Princeton University—developed what was called "Top 40 Radio." After Orson Welles' 1938 "War of the Worlds'" Hallowe'en broadcast successfully convinced 25% of its audience that an invasion of the United States was being carried out in New Jersey, either by "Martian-style" aliens or by Germans, there was unbridled interest in radio's propagandistic potential.

"Top 40" was a "quantitative popular survey," based on the theories of project members Paul Lazarsfeld and T.W. Adorno, of what Americans could most easily be induced to believe they had independently and merely "by popular demand" decided they wanted to hear broadcast several times a day on their radio sets. There was one ironclad uniformity in 1950s and 1960s "Top 40" radio: No musical selection, under nearly any circumstances, played for longer than four minutes. That prohibition structurally eliminated nearly all Classical music from radio play, except through the Saturday broadcasts of the Metropolitan Opera or other forms of "special programming."

This meant that under the guise of an ostensibly potentially infinite variety, a rigid and arbitrary formalism, dedicated primarily to shortening the attention span of attentive listeners, was imposed for decades. This shifted only in the late 1960s, when the "boomer generation," whose tastes had been behaviorally modified and shifted by the project throughout childhood and adolescence, became the commercial powerhouse for recordings purchases. (Recordings replaced, and essentially killed, the American practice of making music in the home, many of which had pianos, for example.)

Under the guise of "the democratic expression of contemporary popular taste," the ulterior purpose was to do exactly what Joseph Goebbels was doing in Nazi Germany as its Minister of Propaganda: harness the powerful and still very new tool of radio for propagandistic purposes, including "immoral support" for the propagation of bizarre behavior, including madness, as "trends," much as we see done on the Internet today.

Members of the Princeton Radio Research Project included:

• Frank Stanton, President of CBS from 1946 until 1971, and chairman of the Rand Corporation from 1961 until 1967

• Gordon Allport, leading representative of Great Britain's Tavistock Institute in the United States

• T.W. Adorno, leading member of the Frankfurt School, former asset of the Communist International (Comintern), and leading proponent of the dead-end "twelve tone system" of the now largely forgotten Arnold Schoenberg

• Paul Lazarsfeld, chairman of the project, often referred to as the "father of American sociology," known for his use of quantitative methods of analysis, a precursor of systems analysis as later practiced at the Rand Corporation and elsewhere. He once was quoted as saying that his goal in sociology was "to produce more Paul Lazarsfelds." He unfortunately succeeded.

T.W. Adorno, who headed the project's Music Department, wrote in his book, *The Philosophy of Modern Music*:

What radical music perceives is the untransfigured suffering of man.... The seismographic registration of traumatic shock becomes, at the same time, the technical structural law of music. It forbids continuity and development. Musical language is polarized according to its extreme; towards gestures of shock resembling bodily convulsions on the one hand, and on the other towards a crystalline standstill of a human being whom anxiety causes to freeze in her tracks.... Modern music sees absolute oblivion as its goal. It is the surviving message of despair from the shipwrecked.

Adorno's "radio research" papers particularly noted the "atomized listening" that could result. The purpose was to create a new form of authoritarian society—not the "Big Brother" warned of by George Orwell's *1984*, but millions of "Little Brothers," a "Lord of the Flies" form of dictatorship—the dictatorship of conformity. "The authoritarian character of today is, without exception, conformist.... In the final analysis, this music tends to become the style for everyone, because it coincides with the man-in-the-street style." The use of rhythm, for example, as an externally imposed, "militaristic" constant, heard in all forms of "popular music" through various forms of pounding, through percussion, bass lines, or drill instructor/cheerleader style screaming in "hip hop," is the clearest expression of the dominance of this dictatorial, authoritarian process.

Furtwängler Was Defending the Truth

Violinist Yehudi Menuhin, born in New York City one hundred years ago, in April 1916, was a unique witness to a decisive moment in the decline of Western culture in the 20th Century, and of Classical music in particular. Menuhin, to his everlasting credit, refused to be part of the Nazi-orchestrated defamation of conductor Wilhelm Furtwängler, which began in 1936 and in fact continued until well after Furtwängler's death in 1953. Menuhin recounts in his autobiography: "Furtwängler's fault, like my own perhaps, was to overestimate the power of music. If he did not expect it to absolve original sin, he did believe it proof against contamination … As director of the Berlin State Opera, he decided, again in 1934, to stage *Mathis der Maler*, knowing that (Paul) Hindemith, a 'decadent' composer, did not officially exist; when Göring cancelled the performance, he resigned.… In 1936 Richard Wagner's daughter Friedelind, who fled Nazi Germany three years later, witnessed a meeting between Hitler and Furtwängler at her mother's Bayreuth home.

"I remember Hitler turning to Furtwängler and telling him that he would have to allow himself to be used by the party for propaganda purposes, and I remember Furtwängler refusing. Hitler got angry and told Furtwängler that in that

Violinist Yehudi Menuhin refused to be part of the Nazi-orchestrated defamation of Wilhelm Furtwängler.

case there would be a concentration camp ready for him. Furtwängler was silent for a moment and then said: 'In that case, Herr Reichschancellor, I will be in very good company.' Apparently Hitler was taken aback by the conductor's defiance, because he went into none of his usual rantings but simply walked away."

Hermann Göring, the second in command of the Third Reich, directly orchestrated a campaign to prevent Furtwängler from succeeding Arturo Toscanini at the New York Philharmonic in 1936. In this campaign Göring maliciously instigated a stampede of defamation and cowardice, manipulating international press and influentials, including several Jewish institutions and organizations in New York City, in order to deny Furtwängler that position. The campaign was successful, and Furtwängler was forced to withdraw from the appointment in 1937.

As in a recent, similar act of courage in the facade of barbarism, that of the martyred Syrian archaeologist Khaled al-Asaad, "one of the most important pioneers in Syrian archeology in the 20th Century," Furtwängler defied Hitler to his face, at risk of death, and thereby personified the true Germany, rather than

Hitler, at a time when no one else could have done so, and precisely because no one else then living, understood the soul-elevating power of the inner life of music as Furtwängler did.

Music, like science under the dictatorship of Bertrand Russell, had been killed at the beginning of the 20th Century. It was not naivety that characterized Furtwängler's decisions, but a higher ideal of a society, culture, and music, that did not exist—Germany had been killed—but which Furtwängler preserved for future resurrection, by embodying the truth of, rather than the desecration of Classical culture, as only he was exceptionally equipped to do. Having been denied the American appointment by a Nazi intelligence operation that worked, he stayed in Germany for the same reason that Socrates stayed in Athens and Thomas More stayed in England—under risk of the death that came to both of them, but not to him. His decision was correct.

Toscanini, who, though he had said in 1936 that the only conductor "worthy to replace him" was Furtwängler, denounced Furtwängler as a Nazi sympathizer afterwards. Yet Furtwängler had never committed the mistake in judgement that Toscanini had made in 1919, when he became a Fascist candidate, although he opposed Mussolini later.

Could a faithful and profound lover of the truth contained in the inner life of Classical music have made that mistake? Furtwängler's *musical* criticism of Toscanini, reveals the moral problem at the root of the past 125 years of collapse in Classical culture and science.

"In contrast to, say Nikisch, [Toscanini] has no innate musical talent, and what he does have has been fought for and worked upon. But certain striking shortcomings have remained, above all the enormous waste of space in the forte. The size of his beat in the 'f' is such that it makes any differentiation impossible. As a result, these tuttis are all the same, they sound noisy and

Herman Göring, the second in command of the Third Reich, directly orchestrated a campaign to prevent Furtwängler from succeeding Arturo Toscanini at the New York Philharmonic in 1936.

Arturo Toscanini, who had said in 1936 that Furtwängler was the only conductor qualified to replace him, later denounced Furtwängler as a Nazi sympathizer, despite the fact that Toscanini himself had been a Fascist candidate in 1919 who later rejected Mussolini.

are always at the same volume, and the conductor's ability to bring out differences within the forte, in the lower or middle range or even in important major parts, is quite minimal.

"Toscanini believes what he says, that he plays, as far as possible, literally and in a disciplined manner—not superior and not rational—but still himself and the orchestra.

"His greatness lies in his character. This helps him in the eyes of the world, but it does not, unfortunately, help art. One can say with certainty that if he were a greater artist, if he had deeper insights, a livelier imagination, greater warmth, and devotion to the work, he would not have become so disciplined. And that is why his success is disastrous.

"Those of us who hold great music close to our hearts can never replace true artists with prima donnas and others who are just as disciplined, even if they appear in the sheep's clothing of literal rendering. The view, previously held unconsciously in Germany, that inspiration and understanding in art are more important than discipline and autocratic behavior, is still correct."

The late Yehudi Menuhin can rest assured: neither he, nor Furtwängler, overestimated the power of music. It is simply necessary, and militantly so, to properly estimate the "barbarians at the gate" who seek to subjugate humanity through "treasons, stratagems and spoils" by denying children, such as the young prodigy Menuhin, the music that arms them to free humanity from its persistent proclivity to revert to dark ages, including today.

Achieving the Power of Music

The following dialogue addresses concretely this question of the power of music. It identifies the necessity of, and method for the instruction of young people in the art of *bel canto* voice placement, to achieve that power. It is an excerpt of a conversation between Lynn Yen, Executive Director of the Foundation for the Revival of Classical Culture, and Carmela Altamura, soprano, vocal coach, and co-founder of Inter-Cities Performing Arts, Inc., and the Altamura/Caruso International Voice Competition.

Lynn Yen: The collapse in the speaking of the English language that has occurred . . .

Carmela Altamura: It's all in the speaking! The art *starts* with the speaking . . .

Yen: That is easily heard if you even play the

Lynn Yen, Executive Director of the Foundation for the Revival of Classical Culture.

Carmela Altamura, soprano, vocal coach, and co-founder of Inter-Cities Performing Arts, Inc., and the Altamura/Caruso International Voice Competition.

Schiller Institute

speeches of John F. Kennedy, and compare them to any speech you hear [today].

Altamura: I am constantly ... [she then describes a student who is taking acting lessons]. And he's quite good. He's using me as a sounding board. And I say, "No, no, no—your diction. Your *diction*. You do too much work. And then, your jaw is too tight. I cannot understand. Speak on the vowels, speak on the vowels! Follow the accents! Follow the accents where they normally fall." My God, it takes me forever.

Yen: This has created a circumstance where the culture's degeneration is accelerating at an accelerating rate.

Altamura: Everything has accelerated in degenerating at an accelerating rate. I'm so glad you pick it up.

Yen: It's our view that the only efficient means to address this at this point ...

Altamura: Is the *bel canto* singing.

Yen: That's right. It's the only possible way.

Altamura: The *only* way.

Yen: So we don't find resistance among young people ...

Altamura: But the teachers! They're *ignorant!*

Yen: Yes, yes.

EIRNS/Stuart Lewis

Altamura: They're very ignorant.

Yen: So the bad *good* situation that you have now, is that because there is so much chaos in the educational system, they let anyone walk in who has any semblance of a good idea, and has a positive rapport with the students ... What we need, I believe, is a certain kind of proof of principle, taking a selection of young students and demonstrating that we can essentially, in a relatively short period of time, bring them to a higher level of enunciation of an idea ...

Altamura: The *articulation* of it, yes.

Yen: And so to accomplish this, what we first did was we began the process of people studying the Handel *Messiah*, but not because it was an English text, but that *since* it was an English text, people could not complain that they could not understand what it meant. But the English that they speak ...

Altamura: The *vowel formation* in the speaking range, is Italian, no matter what you are singing.

Yen: Right!

Altamura: No matter *what* language. Whether it's Chinese, whether it's Japanese, whether it's Russian. The vowel formation ... The great singers always have that formation. It involves the passage and the registers. Once you pass the registers, you can no longer make it—you can *think* it.

Yen: Aha! I see ...

Altamura: The mind is the one that tells the vocal chords how much tension to have. Everything is done by the ... And it has to look effortless, no effort at all. And the mind commands the vocal chords, which are very tiny, to tense up, just sufficient to ... Imagine how magnificent God made us to do this. And this mind that hears that note, and is why I make everyone study *slowly*, so that their heart in gets refined and developed. Everybody wants to sing fast, "fast food." I say, "Wait a minute! Wait a minute! You know, give your muscles a chance."

If you're doing an interval from C to D, that's a short distance. but if you're doing an interval C to A, the sixth, it's longer. It takes more time. The brain is ... It takes time to enunciate. Everything is longer. [Sings the interval twice, differently.] That's why [contemporary singers] don't space well. They don't space the melodies well. And you can always know when someone is really professional [that way]. The singers have to become instrumental, and the instrumentalists have to become singers.

Yen: Exactly.

Altamura: Please forgive me if I am boring you with all this but I see that you are on the right road.

Yen: No, this is it. We are, you see, we are sneaking up on people. We don't want to simply say, because it's not exactly true, that "You are hopelessly illiterate."

What we want people to experience is, "We can do this much better." And if you do it much better, if you *sound* better ...

Altamura: It's quality! It's quality! And every voice, no matter what God created, *has its inherent quality, if it is trained properly*. Whether it is chamber, whether it is oratorio, whether it is opera, operetta, we look for the highest quality that you can produce. And most people today, it's all *approximate pitch*. They sing, but it's never *on* pitch. It's approximate. It drives me insane. [Sings several inexact intervals]. I mean, please! It drives me insane! Everything is approximate. No, it's *not* approximate! The axis that hold the world together spins mathematically. Everything is order.

Yen: And this notion of resonance at the proper tuning, which is why Verdi fought for it. So, if you can establish this as a principle in the mind of a student, then, and *only* then, can the student actually understand the concept of the truth.

Altamura: But you know ... we have to expose them to the highest excellence. Because they demand so little of themselves. We have to raise the bar. We have accepted such garbage as art today. I mean, it's an excuse to get attention.

Yen: It's horrible. You see it at Carnegie Hall, at Lincoln Center ... In fact, that's where it's the worst!

Altamura: And that is shocking!

Yen: There, they keep on *lowering* the bar. And the audience is ignorant.

Altamura: They cannot distinguish between amusement, entertainment, and art. There are three distinctions. You may fall into that, but be excellent even in *that!* And then there is the narrow highway of the excellence of the true art. It takes a lot of time and longer preparation. Many are called but few are chosen. Because it takes extraordinary love to do it. And you have to forget about being comfortable and having money, and all this business. It will come to you. God gives us the means to accomplish that for which he called us. As long as we seek... "Seek ye first the kingdom of heaven, and all things will be added unto you." The kingdom is excellence... We cannot give [the students] to make them afraid either, but raise the bar day by day—a little bit higher, a little bit higher. They climb the mountain without even knowing it! And then, all of a sudden, they look back: "Is that *me?*"

EDITORIAL

For a National Space Day

Kesha Rogers addressed NASA Veterans and others in Houston on the 55th Anniversary of Americans in space, May 5, 2016.

Good evening everyone! I want to welcome those of you who are here today on behalf of the Schiller Institute, and thank you for joining us tonight. My name is Kesha Rogers, and I am a former Democratic nominee for Congress and member of the LaRouche PAC Policy Committee.

I continue to campaign nationally in the efforts to defend our space program against egregious attacks and the cuts in funding, including our manned space program. I continue to rally the scientific community and the population, starting with those who witnessed and were engaged—to the great benefit of the country and the world—in the developments of our space program, and have been inspired by the space program. I want to rally the scientific community to again be an inspiration to Americans and to the world in advancing the fight for our future in space.

After these brief remarks, the plan for tonight is just to get feedback from all of you—to have members of the scientific community and the others who are here tonight, particularly the scientific community, share your experiences and say what we can do to inspire the population again to recognize that the space program is our future, and that we desperately need to save it and bring it back again.

I hope this meeting will be a stepping stone to something much greater: I would like to have a larger conference to advocate a National Space Day here in the United States, centered around our first Moon landing. So we have to go out and organize the population and our political figures as to why that is absolutely critical today.

We are here tonight to celebrate a great achievement 55 years ago today. Today is the anniversary of the beginning of America's venture into space. As many of you know, May 5, 1961 was the day that American astronaut Alan Shepard made a 15-minute suborbital flight into space on the Freedom 7 spacecraft. He was the second man in space, following Russian cosmonaut Yuri Gagarin.

Shepard had been chosen as one of the first seven astronauts for NASA, who were brought into the Mercury 7 mission. The mission was announced on April 9, 1957. Probably most of you in this room can name the other six astronauts. Anyone in this room who worked with any of the seven,— I would like to hear those stories.

Without Vision, the People Perish

We inspired Americans, and we inspired the world. On April 9, 1957, when the Mercury 7 mission was announced on national television, it was a great stepping stone for all the world to see. When John Glenn became the first American in Earth orbit in 1962, there again, the population was there to see and celebrate. And the remarkable feat that came about from all of the accomplishments and hard work and commitment to this great vision—and to the great visionaries—was that America became the first to land a man on the Moon. Despite all the odds, we realized the challenge of President John F. Kennedy on July 20, 1969. Kennedy had called for landing a man on the Moon and returning him safely to Earth. This is something, again, that the entire world rejoiced in, and it was looked at as a great advance for all of mankind.

So I find again, that it's very fitting, for people who don't know, that when the Apollo 11 mission—of Neil

Armstrong, Buzz Aldrin, and one of my favorites, Michael Collins (whom we don't want to leave out!)—went to the Moon, the plaque that the astronauts left there read: "We came in peace for all mankind."

That should be, once again, our mission, to come in peace for all mankind. And that should be the mission of our space program.

In a statement published in our *Executive Intelligence Review*, titled "A Unified Mission for the Common Aims of Mankind," I call on the scientific community to restore its commitment to the future of our nation in the exploration of space. This is not going to be done with cheap gimmicks, but only through real leadership. There are a lot of cheap gimmicks going on out there; people want to make side-cuts, thinking that we can turn the space program into some kind of marketplace, or going into space and making it a tourist attraction or amusement park. And that is not what our space program represents.

We need the type of leadership to fight for our space program that President John F. Kennedy represented, or visionary leaders like Krafft Ehricke, who was a great space pioneer, and someone whom I often mention, who recognized that space was a mission for mankind: That it was our prerogative, and our duty to our own species, to advance beyond Earth and go out into the Solar System, because this is where we are going to learn how to improve our conditions here on planet Earth and how to better understand our own creative powers as human beings. Because, as Ehricke said, there is nothing and no one under the stars, that can put limitations on mankind, except mankind himself. And I think that is absolutely true: We have to stop putting the limitations on ourselves, and to actually start to move forward with our mission in the conquest of space.

Kennedy said, quoting *Proverbs* 29, that where there is no vision the people perish. Now, I have to tell you, "perishing" is just the direction we are heading in under this collapsing financial system, and under the direction of the current administration—the collapsing trans-Atlantic financial system and the push for total war and chaos that we're seeing right now.

Right now we are in a complete slide into war. We are continuing the escalation toward war against some of our great allies—against China, by putting aircraft carriers and missile defense systems right on its borders and on the borders of Russia. This is a problem! Because we should be committing ourselves to collaborating as human beings, in the fight for increasing the understanding of who we are as human beings.

And that is what the space program represents. It's very interesting that on April 24, China celebrated its first National Space Day, joining with Russia, which celebrates on April 12 the first man in space, Yuri Gagarin. As I said in my statement, the United States right now is "spaced out." We don't have a Space Day, we have people who are completely spaced out. [laughter]

We do not remember that our nation was once an inspiration for the world! Now, we're bullies to the world and the world is afraid of us, because instead of inspiring, we're starting wars, causing economic collapse, and wanting to be the great hegemonic world power. And that's not what the United States represented under the vision of Kennedy or Franklin Roosevelt, or that of our Founding Fathers and Alexander Hamilton. That's the nation we need again today.

Why a National Space Day?

Why is it that China and Russia have a Space Day? It is not just to celebrate an individual event or an individual person. They are celebrating their respective national Space Days because they want to celebrate the achievements of a nation and its commitment to the future of mankind, to those children not yet born, to the advances in science that have yet to be made, the advances and discoveries that still await us. That is why we must have a National Space Day.

What we have already achieved is the landing of a man on the Moon. Now China is going to do something even more remarkable: It is going to be the first nation to put a spacecraft on the far side of the Moon. Think about that one! They're calling for the development of helium-3 mining on the Moon. The United States has to renew its commitment. China's announcement of its plan to land a spacecraft on the far side of the Moon should be a wake-up call to the United States that we should be joining in this effort. But we have insane politicians who say we shouldn't be working with China in space. This is going to set us back a long way! We've got to push for leadership to fight now to reverse the policy that the United States should not be working with nations such as China.

I have just been reading Gene Kranz's book. If you haven't seen this, it is very,— it's called *Failure Is Not an Option: Mission Control from Mercury to Apollo and Beyond*. In this book, Kranz is talking about the commitment and the fight led by members of our space program at the time, in the Apollo mission and so forth, against the ending of the Apollo mission. And against those who said then, as they do today, "Oh, we don't have the resources for that, we don't have the money to go into space."

You know, that's just all lies! Because we have the money to build more nuclear arsenal, we have billions of dollars for more bailouts for the financial looters, and we have money for more wars. And, as you know, when the Apollo mission was being attacked, we were increasing spending on the Vietnam War, which itself was taking away the vision. This came about in the wake of the assassination of President John F. Kennedy.

After President Kennedy was killed, there was a fight to keep his commitment alive. But today we see that it's been completely ripped apart. China is now committing itself to landing on the far side of the Moon. Do you guys know that we had this as a mission? There were people working with Kranz, working with former astronaut Harrison Schmitt, who were actually putting together plans for the United States to be the first to land on the far side of the Moon! Schmitt, of the Apollo 17 mission, was one of the leading advocates for the United States to do this and for the United States to realize the importance of mining helium-3 on the Moon.

'I Felt Betrayed'

But those efforts were defeated. And given the direction in which we are now going, under the current policy of the administration, it may not be able to be realized. We have to actually fight for a commitment to a unified national mission again. The Moon is just the place to do that. Most nations right now recognize that, including India, which has just also announced its commitment to development and research for mining of helium-3 on the Moon. And most nations recognize that the development of the lunar surface, as I said, is the key to the success of *any* type of further mission in space, including the Mars mission, or a mission to any other planetary body.

I have a paragraph from Gene Kranz's book that I want to read. In the course of describing the fight around the ending of the Apollo mission, Kranz says:

> The space program was also suffering. The lunar program was coming to an end. With the cancellations of the last Apollo missions—18, 19, and 20—I felt betrayed. It was as if Congress was ripping our heart out, gutting the program we had fought so hard to build. Leadership is fragile. It is more a matter of mind and heart than resources, and it seemed that we no longer had the heart for those things that demanded discipline, commitment, and risk.

It is very true today. There are many new developments—in terms of the direction the world is taking right now—that I can speak on today, and there are probably some that you here can tell me about as well. Particularly regarding nations like China, Russia, and India, that have committed themselves to the advance of mankind in space,— this is the economic driver for the world. This has to be the economic driver once again for the United States. And I think we have to realize that it is in our national interest and the interest of the world that we, the United States, commit ourselves again to a unified national mission in the exploration of space. I think that we can do it, if we just choose to fight.

So I will stop there. What I hope to hear from you is where you see the future of our nation, and how we can actually come together and make sure that we rally the American people to recognize that this is their future. This is not just some side issue here. It is something that I have been fighting for, for some time— probably not as long as some of you. We need to get people to realize that the whole political spectrum right now is just a joke! If you are not talking about this, if there are not meetings and discussions from political candidates, the Presidential candidates, about the future of our nation in space, what are you talking about?

So that's what we should discuss here today, and I think the message will get around. And you should tell all your friends, "Hey, somebody's fighting." So, what do you have?